IMAGES
of Ireland

ENNISCORTHY

A FLOURISHING RIVER TRADE, *c.* 1880. This is one of the best known views of Enniscorthy. Alas, the scene has changed considerably. Modernisation and growth have enlarged the town and the ways of a bygone era are no more than a photographic memory. Gone are the famous Slaney gabbards or cots that tied up along the quayside. There was a once flourishing river trade here and each side of the river was lined by fine warehouses.

IMAGES
of Ireland

ENNISCORTHY

Compiled by
Dan Walsh

GILL & MACMILLAN

Published in Ireland by
Gill & Macmillan Ltd
Goldenbridge, Dublin 8
with associated companies throughout the world
© Dan Walsh, 1998
0 7171 2771 0

Published in Great Britain by
The Chalford Publishing Company
Printed by
Bailey Print, Dursley, Gloucestershire

Also published in the *Images of Ireland* series:
Banbridge (Angela Dillon)
East Belfast (Keith Haines)
Tralee (Kathleen Brown)

QUAYS AND TURRET ROCK, *c.* 1920. The Turret Rock acts as a superb backdrop to the town of Enniscorthy.

Contents

THE SLANEY RIVER AND BRIDGE, *c.* 1965. The building on the far quayside was the old public toilets. In the background the spires of St Mary's church, Enniscorthy Castle and St Aidan's cathedral dominate the skyline.

THE RIVER SLANEY, *c.* 1965. Not a cot in sight, just a tranquil river. The quays dating from the 1840s are prominent, and in the centre are the ESB offices, established in 1925 as The Electricity Committee and only removed to make way for the new bridge in the past decade!

Introduction

Not for the first time in its long and distinguished history, Enniscorthy is the focus of national and international attention in this year of the 1798 bicentenary commemorations. It is therefore natural to assume, and most appropriate, that this famous Co. Wexford town should be featured in the Images of Ireland series.

I know it is a well worn cliché, but it is true to say that 'a picture is worth a thousand words'. Each picture has its own story to tell and captures a mood and a character that is unique, revealing what is nostalgic, industrious and progressive; each one a symbol of a bygone moment.

Enniscorthy's past has been important to the town's good name and could be a vital asset in the years ahead as greater emphasis is placed on tourism. Long established is its proud reputation as the location for the midsummer Co. Wexford Strawberry Fair, synonymous with delicious succulent fruit and an unforgettable festival atmosphere. Equally well established is the town's significant place in Irish history.

In 1798 the Wexford pikemen rose in defence at Vinegar Hill and again, in 1916, Enniscorthy was the only town outside Dublin that seriously supported the Easter Rising. Even though the events of 1798 happened too early for photography, the men and women of 1916 are remembered in the section devoted to Public Service.

Enniscorthy's industrial past was supported by a rich agricultural hinterland and consequently, flour manufacture, the conversion of barley into malt and other farming related activities were the key to its success. As a market town it had few rivals and was the envy of many bigger and more prosperous centres.

This book also extends into rural Enniscorthy and remembers the great days of the landlords at Wilton Castle, Solsborough, Brownswood, Borodale, Castleboro and other great houses. Also remembered is P.J. Roche, the man who saved Enniscorthy Castle from certain destruction nearly a century ago, as well as others who used their entrepreneurial skills to create employment and enterprise in the area.

Included too are photographic records of many presidential visits, Eamon de Valera, Erskine Childers and, the most famous and best loved Irish President to date, Mary Robinson. The fact that all three visited Enniscorthy on special occasions reflects the importance of Enniscorthy and its people in the hearts and minds of many of the nation's first citizens.

Since the invention of the camera, Enniscorthy has been a magnet for photographers, and why not? Just look at the breath-taking scenery of the old days! The famous P.A. Crane Collection, now under the stewardship of Ibar Carty, is one of the best archives in the country. Ken Hemmingway's amazing postcard collection is an invaluable source and he has readily made it available for inclusion in this work. Others, like Paddy Murphy and Christy Doyle, have preserved a more recent vintage. Enniscorthy Camera Club continues to make a contribution that will be important in the distant future.

In this book I have tried to present the best of Enniscorthy photography, bearing in mind the material made available to me. The quality has also been a vital factor, and I have been careful to exclude nobody. You will find therefore, references to everybody, from the gentry to the ordinary folk.

The precious photographs in this compilation are a part of Enniscorthy's history. The town is constantly changing. Many new buildings are being erected, the population is growing, and the future is going to be very different from the romantic pedestrian ways of the past.

Acknowledgements

Naturally a publication of this type would be impossible to compile without the co-operation and goodwill of many of the town's people. It is equally logical that any hope of thanking everybody individually is out of the question.

However, I sincerely appreciate the efforts of everybody, no matter how small, from those who loaned many photographs to those who named some of the people in photographs who were difficult to identify.

I would like to give a special mention to Archdeacon K.S. Wilkinson, Ken Hemmingway, Christy Doyle, Paddy Murphy (photographer), Paddy Murphy (potter), Flo and Bill Peare, Ned Fenlon, David Carberry of the County Museum, Adrian King of IFA, Sydney Murphy, Martin Murphy, Mick Quigley, Harry Kehoe, Denis Doyle, Mrs Dorothy Owens, Brian Cleare, Seamus Rafter, David Hasslacher and Anne Carroll.

I also sincerely appreciate Ibar Carty's permission to use prints from the valuable archive of P.A. Crane, especially the fine study of St Patrick's Day, 1952, in Enniscorthy's Market Square, which adorns the cover of this publication.

One
Sights and Scenes

BROWNSWOOD CASTLE, *c.* 1890. The Cromwellians destroyed this fine castle in 1650, but the ruin seen here has remained unchanged to this day and is a well known landmark for users of the busy N11, which carries traffic between Rosslare Port and Dublin. Across the river can be seen Borrmount House, which was built by James Gethings in 1841 and is now the property of local farmer, Pat Doyle.

CASTLE STREET, *c*. 1940. The Athenaeum, or town hall, has dominated Castle Street since it was built by local contractor, Michael Lynch, in 1892. The hall played host to the great Irish tenor, Count John McCormack and it was on its stairs that Ireland's foremost theatrical duo, Hilton Edwards and Liam MacLiammoir, first met. In 1916, leader Padraig Pearse delivered an oration from the stage, two months before his execution, and when the Irish Volunteers rose in Enniscorthy in 1916, they acquired the Athenaeum as their headquarters and raised the tricolour above the building.

RAFTER STREET, *c*. 1965. Long before the days of one-way streets, Rafter Street took on a relaxed appearance. Thornton's chemist on the left, the Home & Colonial Stores and John Cullen's boot shop on the right, are no longer with us. Burke-O'Leary's, beside Thornton's, is the oldest drapery business in the town, with origins traced back to the 1840s.

CASTLE STREET, *c.* 1915. This house stood beside the National Bank (opened in 1835) and in the 1860s served as a residence for the Mission Fathers before they moved across the river to a modern site overlooking the town. Once the business premises of Mr Keane, the shop front is typical of Enniscorthy at the time. It was later completely demolished to make way for the Church Institute.

MARKET SQUARE, *c.* 1936. There are few cars and there is no one-way traffic system. Thornton's on the corner was the pioneer in the domestic photographic processing business. The Home & Colonial Stores were the nearest thing that shoppers got to the supermarket in those days. Centre stage is the famous 1798 memorial and to the right is the Technical Institute building, better known today as the Urban Council administration offices.

CASTLE HILL, 1904 (above left). Nestling in the shadow of Enniscorthy Castle is McDermott's Furniture Warehouse where a well made table and a set of chairs await public attention. The family shop also specialised in china, glass and earthenware products. Master carpenter Albert McDermott died in 1944. NEW COOKER AT ENNISCORTHY CASTLE, 1904 (above right). This splendid example of modern engineering was installed in the kitchen at Enniscorthy Castle by the Roches as part of the extensive renovations that occurred before the family took up residence. The ovens are marked 'roasting' on the left and 'baking' on the right. Fuelled by coal, it bears the makers name, 'John Sinnott & Sons, Wexford', who were wholesale and retail ironmongers. They had plumbing warehouses in Wexford town for about a century, before closing down in the 1950s.

MARKET SQUARE, c.1905. Carts are parked in the centre while a donkey is safely anchored to a special pen – no question of congestion then, in the mud-laid street. The row of business premises in the centre are uniform, in every way – all three storey, all the same size, with identical shopfronts and one continuous roof. This pattern was broken when the sites of Nos 3 and 4 were converted into a modern bank.

THE OLD STONE BRIDGE, *c.* 1965. With the historic Vinegar Hill and the remnants of the old quayside warehouses rising up in the background, the old stone bridge signifies Enniscorthy's heritage and history.

ENNISCORTHY TOWN, 1926. The town was compact with many prominent buildings when this view was taken from Vinegar Hill. The rural hinterland that serves as an attractive backdrop was the general heartland that supplied the agricultural economy upon which the success of the town depended.

ENNISCORTHY QUAYS, 1914. The site of the Allied Irish Bank is only a garden today. Across the river Slaney with its cots in dock, the quayside buildings are dwarfed by the large chimney stack that rose above the margarine factory, later Earle's bakery. The buildings to the immediate right served Copeland's cash and carry business as well as a private residence.

AERIAL VIEW, c. 1965. As the river Slaney winds towards Wexford the Co-op buildings dominate the foreground, but of tremendous interest is the town gasometer in the centre. The health clinic site is just a plain field and the twin sheds (later to serve as the fire station) mark the spot where the first commercial timber garden sheds were manufactured by Barna Buildings Ltd.

A WEXFORD COT, c. 1940. The Slaney was once one of Ireland's busiest rivers, with a fleet of characteristic cots plying between the port of Wexford and the villages of Castlebridge to Enniscorthy. Cots is an Irish term meaning 'a small boat', but the Slaney cots were substantial craft which could carry about 80 tons of cargo.

THE COTMEN, c. 1940. The cot trade on the Slaney offered plenty of well paid employment. Usually four voyages a week were made to Enniscorthy. Huge quantities of maize were imported from Liverpool to Wexford port where they were discharged and shipped by cot to Enniscorthy. Coal, slates, fertilisers, cement and other goods were also transported to the town, while the downward cargoes consisted mainly of maize-meal and pollard from Davis's flour mills.

TEMPLESHANNON QUAY, *c.*1915. A three storey Georgian building on Enniscorthy Quay, this was a substantial building. When owned by Mr Pettigrew it became the first residence of four Mission Fathers on 17 October 1866.

THE COFFEE HOUSE, *c.* 1940. Affectionately known as 'the Coffee House' this quaint and curious building stood as a landmark at the pinnacle of the Turret Rocks overlooking the town. It was built by a Quaker merchant and Enniscorthy Town Commissioners' member, Joshua Bobiar, in 1840, as a summer retreat where he entertained family and friends in exclusive surroundings. It passed into the ownership of the House of Missions and was occupied by several tenants before it was demolished in the mid 1960s.

PORTSMOUTH ARMS HOTEL, *c.* 1962. As Enniscorthy's oldest and most popular hotel, it was the haunt of commercial travellers and early tourists. It was the meeting place of many generations, just like Enniscorthy bridge. The hotel was established as a coaching inn in 1796. It played host to many famous people including President Eamon de Valera, Eamon Andrews and Gay Byrne. Between 1882 and 1964 it was run by three generations of the Bennett family. Afterwards it had a succession of owners and many misfortunes, including a number of fires. Consequently, while in a neglected condition, it was demolished by order of Enniscorthy Urban Council in 1976.

DEMOLITION OF THE PORTSMOUTH ARMS, 1976.

ENNISCORTHY POST OFFICE, 1918. This red brick, two storey building first opened its doors on 4 May 1903. The building contractor was a local man, William Fortune, of Lower Church Street, and the new building cost £2,653 including fitting-out costs. Alterations were made to it in 1909. These alterations were primarily for improved telephone and telegraph access and the sorting office was extended in length by ten feet. The cost was £397. In 1922, £285 was spent on further alterations, including the change of plaque bearing the initials 'ER' to the new Irish symbol, the harp. The post office served as the telephone exchange until 1972 when the 'hello girls' were transferred to a regional centre of operations at Waterford.

ST AIDAN'S PRESBYTERY, 1914. Popularly known as 'The Manse', it was built as a presbytery for the administrator and his curates and was completed in 1909 to coincide with the silver jubilee celebrations for the Most Revd James Browne, Bishop of Ferns, 1884–1918. Inspired by Administrator Fr Robert Fitzhenry, the building was designed by T.F. Slevin & Sons, Dublin, and built by William Fortune of Lower Church Street, Enniscorthy.

ST SENAN'S HOSPITAL, *c.* 1965. Opened in 1865 as the county lunatic asylum, the distinguished red-brick institution became part of folklore. It is rumoured that the plans got mixed up and that St Senan's should have been built somewhere in India! It occupies a prime site on the outskirts of the town.

CHRISTIAN BROTHERS' PRIMARY SCHOOL, *c.* 1965. Opened in 1949, this two storey building became the bastion of education for many bright young Enniscorthymen. It was later incorporated into the post-primary facilities on the site.

VINEGAR HILL, c. 1930. With its famous landmark, the windmill, Vinegar Hill was the scene of major action during the 1798 Rebellion and is famous in history, legend and song. It is a favourite viewing point for visitors and locals alike and affords views all over Co. Wexford and into counties Waterford and Kilkenny.

MILL PARK ROAD, c. 1905. A two storey red-brick residence dominates this entrance to the town from the New Ross side. At the top of the road on the left, are the warehouses of Lett's Brewery. To the immediate right, the fine white-capped brick piers adorn the entrances to St John's Terrace, while O'Neill's Terrace is no more than a planners' dream!

IRISH STREET, c. 1940. People stroll casually and enjoy the hazy sunshine where the leafy trees beautifully frame Irish Street, with the spire of St Aidan's Cathedral rising majestically into the summer sky.

ISLAND ROAD, c. 1960. Today the N11 Euro Route between Rosslare Harbour and Belfast still travels along Island Road, the last streetscape entering or leaving Enniscorthy from the Dublin side – a far cry from the days of this quite and picturesque scene.

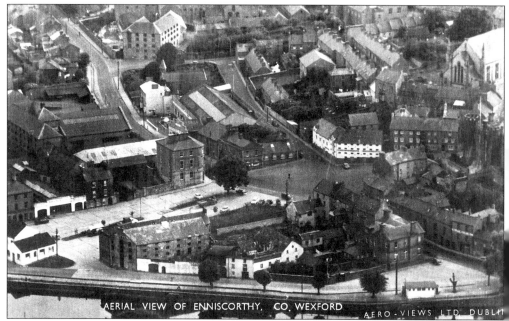

AERIAL VIEW, c. 1965. A well tended tree stands alone at the head of Abbey Square, once home to the great annual Strawberry Fair festival. At the bottom of the Square are the old ESB offices, and immediately on the bottom left are the old Royal Irish constabulary barracks, which served the Garda Siochana from 1921 until 1965.

CORBALLY BRIDGE, 1983. This magnificent triple-arched architectural wonder, which extends 98 ft above the waters of the little Blackwater river, is reckoned to be Ireland's second highest bridge. About 3 miles from Enniscorthy, it carries traffic using the main Enniscorthy to Oulart road. A slate tablet on the bridge reads: 'Corbally Bridge, James B. Farrell Esqr, Engineer Philip Cowman, Contractor, MDCCCLIV' (1854).

CARLEY'S BRIDGE, c. 1910. The river Urrin flows beneath the arches of Carley's Bridge. Visible behind the trees beyond the bridge are the buildings of the old woollen mills, while towards the right is a new row of cottages.

NEW BRIDGE, 1988. A heavy crane was used to replace the railway bridge at Mill Park Road. This was one of many bridges replaced or reconstructed by Iarnroid Eireann.

Cliffe House, Enniscorthy.

CURRY.

CLIFF HOUSE, *c.* 1920. This fine eighteenth century house was built for the mill manager at Davis' flour mills. It enjoys a picturesque view along the Slaney valley in the direction of Wexford. The present owner is Frank Mackin, who is well known in the travel business.

SALVILLE HOUSE, *c.* 1920. Originally built as part of St Senan's Hospital, as the home of the Resident Medical Officer in the late 1860s, it is now in private ownership.

Two
Industry and Business

ST JOHN'S IRONWORKS AND FOUNDRY, *c.* 1955. Thomas Jessop Davis was an engineer by profession and opened St John's ironworks and foundry in the grounds of St John's Mills in the 1890s. He built a new foundry opposite the mill in 1908, which traded successfully until it was closed down in 1962. The foundry carried out such work as casting pillar boxes for the post office and street inspection manhole covers for local authorities.

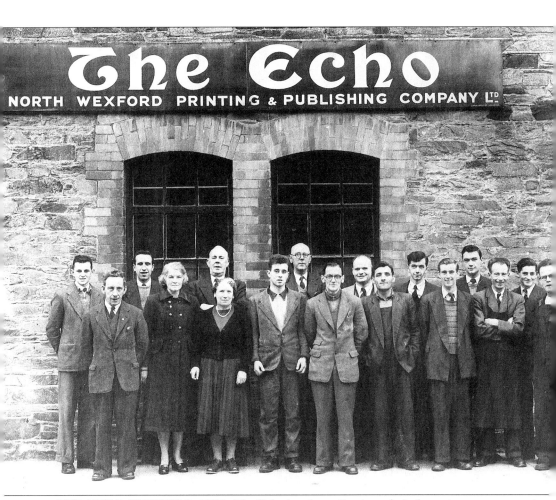

THE ECHO WORKERS, 1957. *The Echo* has been Enniscorthy's favourite newspaper sinc
1902 and has always provided good employment. It is the only newspaper printed in the tow
and generations of workers have produced it from the old days of hot metal to the moder
computerised age. To celebrate the expansion of the premises this group of workers called o
the photographer to make a permanent record. From left to right: Jim Quirke (compositor)
Mickey Nolan (Linotype operator); Johnny Cleary (office worker); Mamie Cooney (binder)
Bill Quirke (Linotype operator); Ciss Lyne (binder); Tom Kearney (delivery-man); Padd
Pierce (Intertype operator); Kevin Bateman (compositor); Kevin McCarthy (Linotyp
operator); David O'Brien (general operative); Michael Donegan (compositor); Ned Fenlo
(general operative); Joe Nolan (compositor); Pat Walsh (compositor); John Foley (journalist
and James 'Dickie' Quirke (machine foreman).

CHO FIRE, 1968. The printing works of *The Echo* at Mill Park Road were completely gutted y a major fire. However, the newspaper did come out that week, with its own disaster story eaming across the front page, thanks to friends in the *Carlow Nationalist*. This photograph ows the printing presses, and foreman, Jim Quirke, covering some of the damaged machinery.

NEW ERA FOR THE ECHO, 1971. With the premises fully refurbished it was time for ormal work to resume for the staff of the newspaper. Ready to dispatch the first issues from a ew printing press were Catherine Crowe (nee Murphy), Catherine McGrath (nee Murphy), reda (nee Leslie), Ciss Lyne, Mary Kate Williams and Mai Murphy.

ST JOHN'S MILLS, *c.* 1920. This extraordinary winter scene shows railway wagons parked i the yard of St John's Mills collecting flour and provisions for transportation around the countr

ST JOHN'S MILLS, *c.* 1965. From a simple watermill in 1858, the mills developed to becom this impressive image of industry and success. The first grain silos were erected in 1935 an added to in 1954, to became a familiar landmark. Run by the Davis family, the mills provide employment for generations of Enniscorthy workers; operations ceased on 30 June 1989.

ST JOHN'S MILLS, 1983. This impressive study of St John's Mills reflects years of successful industry, but the reality was that they would close within a few years.

LETT'S BEST, 1982. Until 1956 beer was brewed by the Lett family at Mill Park Road. In the early 1980s the recipe for the drink was sold to the Coors Beer Company in America. Bill Lett made regular trips to the United States where he appeared in newspapers and on television advertising the Irish product. This unique photograph was used for publicity purposes and shows some of the large posters promoting George Killian's beer in France.

THE POTTER'S CRAFT, c. 1920. Dick Brickley, with generations of tradition in his veins turns out a clay pot. The craft has changed very little to this day.

THE MASTER POTTER, *c.* 1980. In 1979 Paddy Murphy set up his own business called Hillview Potteries. His family, the Brickleys, had origins in Davidstown and left Paddy a legacy of four centuries of tradition in the pottery trade. The craft of turning out quality products has changed very little over the centuries, except that electricity is now used to drive the wheel and modern designs have been added to the range of products.

THE YOUNGEST POT MAKER, *c.* 1990. Paddy Murphy has taught his nephew, Derek O'Rourke, the art of pottery manufacture. Derek became Ireland's 'youngest potter' and exhibited his trade at shows and exhibitions when he was only eight years old!

CARLEY'S BRIDGE BRICKYARD, *c.* 1900. Sam Brickey, with his sons, Tom, Dick and Martin, at work in the large brick making yard at Carley's Bridge. Tens of thousands of red clay bricks were made there and used in the building of the post office and many private residence in the Enniscorthy district.

OPENING THE NEW BRIDGE, 1975. The first bridge to span the river Slaney at Edermine was opened in 1898, but by the early 1960s it was rather the worse for wear. Long campaigning resulted in a new single lane bridge provided by Wexford County Council in the mid 1970s. Legendary All Ireland Hurling star, Nicky Rackard, was on hand to cut the ribbon and declared the Marmion Bridge, named after a local abbott, well and truly open.

O'CONNOR'S FACTORY, c. 1974. Revd Patrick Cummins, Administrator, performs the blessing at the opening of O'Connor's Engineering Company on the Dublin Road. Also in the picture are Fr Philip Doyle (Superior, Mission House), Mrs Maureen O'Connor, Michael O'Leary (Tanaiste), who performed the official opening, Denis O'Connor and his son, Declan.

KINSELLA & MAGUIRE, *c.* 1907. This business occupied a prime location at Templeshannon and is now owned by the Kavanagh family. The distinguished group includes Ned Dillon; John Quirke; Myles Kehoe (who married Annie Sinnott in 1919 and inherited a very successful grocery business and licensed premises at Castle Hill, which he carried on until his death in 1970); Peter Doyle; Tom Maguire (joint proprietor) and on the extreme right, the other proprietor, Morgan Kinsella.

KEHOES OF CASTLE HILL, 1982. Myles and Gabrielle Kehoe show off the best wine at their store on Castle Hill. Myles learned the trade from his father of the same name and took complete control of the business in 1970. With his wife they pioneered the off-licence trade in the town.

MEASURING THE TEA, 1980.
Dessie O'Rourke uses a steady hand to weigh accurately every pound of Manor brand tea at the firm of H. Murphy & Co., Mill Park Road. This was the final stage in local tea production. Such slow and out-dated methods of tea production were being squeezed by competition from tea bags, while health regulations also put pressure on this type of business.

OLD ENNISCORTHY DISAPPEARS, 1989. A bulldozer levels the old Boat Club building at the corner of Abbey Square and Abbey Quay, to make way for the N11 inner road.

MACHINERY YARD, 1960. Some vintage machinery, including steam and road rollers, at the County Council's machinery yard.

THE MACHINERY YARD, 1960. This general view shows the extent of the yard. Outside the wall, it is a family day out, as people used the Promenade for recreation, while to the right is the famous Ball Alley. Everything in this picture was demolished to make way for a new hotel which is currently under construction.

THE END OF THE MACHINERY YARD, 1996. The gate is being locked for the last time at the machinery yard, which had served for many years as the headquarters of Wexford County Council in Enniscorthy. A new hotel is currently being constructed on the site and the staff have moved to temporary premises at the old Fruit Depot at St John's. From left to right: Catherine Coade, Mary Carton, Mary Kehoe, John Dunne, Joe Moorehouse, Bernard Dunne, Pat Kehoe, Tommy Larkin, John Breen, M.J. Rossiter, Pat Cloke, Tom Quigley and Matt Flynn. Christy Doyle, who was behind the lens on this occasion, was the other member of the staff involved in this small slice of local history.

BROWNSWOOD QUARRY, 1960. Seen here is some of the early machinery used for quarrying the rock at Brownswood. It was originally worked by Wexford County Council but was acquired by Roadstone in 1961 and is still used for the same purpose by this very successful semi-state company.

THE FARMER'S PRESIDENT, c. 1974. President of the Irish Farmers' Association, T.J. Maher, later a Member of the European Parliament, is distracted by a well wisher during a visit to Enniscorthy's Farm Centre. Also in the picture (centre) is Charles Deacon, a well known farm activist, historian and author from Clonroche.

JUNIOR CHAMBER, 1974. Chairman of Enniscorthy Urban District Council, Cllr Andy Doyle, makes a presentation to Victor Conlon of Enniscorthy Junior Chamber at a function in the Portsmouth Arms Hotel. Also in the photograph are Mrs Helen Doyle, Mrs V. Conlon, Mr and Mrs Pat Kickham.

PRESIDENT CHILDERS, 1973. His Excellency, The President of Ireland, Mr Erskine Childers, cuts the ribbon at the opening of Enniscorthy Credit Union's new offices at Market Square in the company of Neville James and Seamus Counihan.

WEXFORD IFA, 1974. Members of the National Farmer's Association, later the Irish Farmer's Association, gather in large numbers at Enniscorthy Livestock Market.

PERSON OF THE YEAR, 1974. Donie Askins wins the coveted shield presented by Enniscorthy Junior Chamber. The presentation is made by John Daly. Also in the photograph are, front: Frances Roche (nee Crane) and Liam O'Leary; back: Cllr Denis O'Connor, Jim White, James Symes (Manager, Bank of Ireland), and Tom Kelly.

HAPPY ANNIVERSARY, 1980. Celebrating the 50th anniversary of H. Murphy & Co., Mill Park Road, are management and staff, including: John Canavan; Sydney Murphy (director); Patrick Griffin (cash and carry manager); Herbert Murphy (managing director); Bertie Hayden (dispatch manager), and Sean Sheahan.

ENNISCORTHY BILLHEAD, 1883.

8, 21 & 22, MAIN STREET,
ENNISCORTHY, *April 24* 1883

Mrs Shiell Tomsonid

Bought at PATRICK RYAN'S
HARDWARE,
IRONMONGERY AND FURNISHING WAREHOUSE.
BAR, ROD AND SHEET IRON, STEEL, &c.

1881					
April 2	½ Stone Cow grass	"		16	6
	½ Stone Red Clover	"		4	6
	½ Stone Alsyke	"		6	0
	2 Stone Imported Italian G Sed	"		8	0
	2 Stone Perennial do.	"		7	0
14	1 Do, Bone manure	"		14	0
	2 Stone Perennial G Seed	"		7	0
May 14	½ Stone Cow grass	"		5	6
	1 Stone Perennial Seed	"		3	6
	2 Stone Italian Seed 4½	"		9	0
June 7	5 Bags Bone manure	3	10	0	
July 4	Timber Furnished	1	3	7	
Sept 10	5 naggin Black Japan	"		3	1
	½ Pint Turpentine	"		.	4
	4 lls white Lead	"		1	4
	Lamp Black	"		.	4
	3·12 feet 2×2 Scantling	"		2	6
	1·12 feet 9×3 Deal	"		3	3
	1·0 Bar Iron Lay	"		10	4
	Hoop	"		.	6
	½ Dozen Bolts & nuts	"		1	0
	4 Pair But Hinges	"		1	8
	2 Sash Fasteners	"		1	6
	20 & 6 Batten	"		.	6
16	3 Sash Fasteners	"		2	0
	3 Pair But Hinges	"		1	6
1882	Oil cloth	"		.	9
April 20	2 Stone Cow grass	1	2	0	
	½ Stone Alsyke	"		5	6
	½ Stone Red clover	"		4	6
	3 Stone Italian G Seed	"		13	6
	1½ Stone Perennell "	"		4	6
May 25	5 Bags Bone manure	3	10	0	
		£ 16	5	2	

Apr Paid Ry Case 5 0 0

THE GROCERY HALL,
24, GEORGE'S STREET,
Enniscorthy, *Oct 21* 1889

Mrs Shiell

Bought of EDWARD GOFF,
TEA, WINE AND SPIRIT MERCHANT,
AND PROVISION CURER.
☞ Coffee Roasted by Steam Power, and Ground Daily.

3½ Bacon 5	15	7½
Rtty malt	3	0
Tobaco	1	0
	19	7½

Eds Ed Goff

Janr 29/90

BILLHEAD FROM EDWARD GOFF,
GEORGE STREET (NOW RAFTER
STREET), 1889.

41

MARKET SQUARE,

Enniscorthy, ——— 14/2/ ——— 1884

M.<u>rs</u> Shiell   Tomnull

To J. DOWNES, Dr.

LINEN AND WOOLLEN DRAPERY,
MILLINERY & FANCY WAREHOUSE,
BOOT AND SHOE MANUFACTURER.

				£	s	d
=	Goods				12	11
=	D.o			2	12	7
=	D.o			1	18	0
				£ 5	3	5
Apr. 24	5 Supes	9/-		2	5	0
May 11	3 D.o	9/-		1	7	0
	2 D.o Bone		4/-	1	2	0
June 8	5 Supes	9/-		2	5	0
„ 1	5 Supes	9/-		2	5	0
„ 16	5 D.o Bone		4/-	2	15	0
„ 19	5 D.o D.o		4/-	2	15	0
July „	2 Do 19.o		4/-	1	2	0
				£20	19	5

Bill at Bank
months
15784   £20 19 5

ENNISCORTHY BILLHEAD, 1884.

42

Three
Public Service

ENNISCORTHY FCA, 1967. Back row: Pte Jackie O'Connor, Pte Joe O'Brien, Pte Harry O'Connor, Pte William Canavan, Pte John Sinnott, Pte William Dobbs. Middle row: Cpl Frankie Conway, Cpl David Murphy, Pte Christy Doyle, Cpl Michael O'Brien, Pte Tommy Donnelly, Pte Paddy O'Shea, Cpl Tom Keane. Front row: Cpl Joe Donnelly, Sgt Paddy Doyle, Lt Harry Ringwood, Sgt Jack Freeman and Cpl Mick Quigley.

ST PATRICK'S DAY, 1952. Members of Enniscorthy FCA, with help from some little supporters, lead the parade down Friary Hill and past the old arched entrance to Lett's Brewery. Leading the lads on the right is Tommy Pepper of Ross Road, while on the left can be spotted Harry Costin (Pearse Road), Paddy Doyle (Bellefield) and Sam O'Shea (Pearse Road). Leading the middle group is P.J. O'Loughlin, Company Commander, followed by Denis Byrne, ex Company Comander. The officer out in front is ? Cantwell.

WILSON TROPHY WINNERS, 1984. Enniscorthy C. Company 10th Battalion FCA won the coveted Wilson Trophy competition at St Stephen's military barracks, Kilkenny, for the first time. Back row, from left to right: Sgt Joe Ronan, Sgt Mick Quigley, Cpl Jackie O'Connor, Pte Tom Davis, Pte Denis Doyle, Pte Andy Murphy, Company Comander Joe O'Brien. Front row: Pte Larry Tinney, Pte Liam Martin, Pte Thomas Dempsey, Pte William Brookes, Pte Joe O'Connor and Pte Richard Martin.

ENNISCORTHY CAMERA CLUB, 1988. Prize-giving time at Enniscorthy Camera Club, with plenty of prizes for everybody. Back row: Christy Doyle, Joan Healy, Ken Hemmingway, Robert Rackard, Matty Coady. Front row: Aidan Quirke, Cllr Sean Sheahan (Chairman, Enniscorthy Urban Council), John Wilkinson and the adjudicator.

ARRIVAL OF NEW FIRE TENDER, *c.* 1969. Enniscorthy's fire fighters turn out in helmet and uniform to show off the new Commer fire tender which was added to the fleet by Wexford County Council. They were photographed in the yard of the old fire station at Mill Park Road which was the headquarters of Enniscorthy Fire Service from 1966 until the new station at Lymington Road was opened twenty years later. The site of the old fire station now contains the ten houses that comprise the Mill Yard Housing Estate. The men are, from left to right: Jim Conroy, Pat Conroy, Tom O'Brien, Tom O'Connor, Andy O'Leary, Jim Sullivan, Paddy Wildes, Joe Cash, Jim Doyle, Marks Redmond and Pat Carley.

FIREMEN'S REUNION, 1972. Members of Enniscorthy Fire Brigade took a night off-duty to attend the annual dinner dance in Murphy-Flood's Hotel. Back row: Mark Redmond, Joe Cash, Pat Carley, Jim Sullivan, Jim Doyle, Paddy Wildes Front row: Andy O'Leary, Tommy O'Connor, Jim Conroy, Pat Conroy, Jack Murphy and Tom O'Brien.

FIRST DAY COVER, 1987. The 75th anniversary commemorations of the first flight across St George's Channel from Fishguard to Crane, near Enniscorthy, by Denis Corbett-Wilson. Des McCarthy, Postmaster at Enniscorthy Post Office, hands over a first day postage cover to Malcolm Cullen of the Corbett-Wilson Committee in Wales.

CORBETT-WILSON PLAQUE, 1987. At the unveiling of a plaque to mark the historic Corbett-Wilson flight in the grounds of the County Museum are -?-, Noel Dillon (County Manager), Cllr Sam McCauley, Revd Thomas Eustace (Administrator, St Aidan's Cathedral), Mrs Mary Yates, Cllr Andy Doyle, Fintan Murphy (Curator of the County Museum), Martin Whelan (Enniscorthy Urban Council), Cllr Peter Byrne, Cllr Paddy Wildes, Cllr Sean Doyle (Chairman of Enniscorthy Urban District Council), Terry Byrne (Public Relations, Aer Lingus), Donal Minnock (Town Clerk, Enniscorthy), Tommy Cranitch and a female relative of Corbett-Wilson.

To commemorate
the first aeroplane flight
between **BRITAIN** and **IRELAND**
by **DENYS CORBETT WILSON**.
His **BLERIOT XI** Landed
in this townsland of **CRANE** on April 22nd 1912.
ERECTED BY CORBETT WILSON COMMITTEE APRIL 22nd 1987.

AN UNVEILING AT CRANE , 1987. Cllr Rory Murphy, Chairman of Wexford County Council, unveils a memorial to Denys Corbett-Wilson on the site at Crane, where he crash landed after his historic flight from Fishguard in 1912. Pictured are Michael Kavanagh (committee member); Dr Michael Corbett-Asby (relative of the airman); Dan Walsh (chairman of the organising committee); John Murphy (secretary of the organising committee); Billy Quirke (committee member); Malcolm Cullen (Chairman of the Corbett-Wilson Committee in Haverfordwest); Terry Byrne (Aer Lingus) and Pat Doyle (committee member).

THE NEW ZEALAND PREMIER, 1993. The Prime Minister of New Zealand, the Right Hon Jim Bolger, whose parents hailed from North Wexford, paid a visit to Bellefield G.A.A. Park for a senior hurling tournament where he met the captains of both teams, Nicky English (Tipperary) and Tom Dempsey (Wexford).

THE VISITORS' BOOK, 1993. The Right Hon Jim Bolger signing the Distinguished Visitors' Book at the Urban Council offices with Chairman, Cllr Paddy Wildes. They are flanked by Cllr Andy Doyle and Mrs Bolger. Back row, from left to right: Cllr John Murphy, Donal Minnock (Town Clerk), Cllr Peter Byrne, Cllr Judy Browne, Cllr Charlie Kavanagh, William Creedon (County Secretary), Anne and Michael Doyle.

PRESIDENT ROBINSON, 1993. During her visit to the County Wexford Community Workshop, President Mary Robinson paid an official visit to the Chambers of Enniscorthy Urban District Council and signed the visitor's book, witnessed by the Chairman, Cllr Paddy Wildes.

MEETING THE PRESIDENT, 1992. The President of Ireland, Her Excellency, Mary Robinson on her only visit to Enniscorthy on 13 September where she officially opened a new extension at the County Wexford Community Workshop in Bellefield. Here she pays a compliment to the Loch Garman Silver Band through the musical director, John Clancy, while in the background her husband, Mr Nick Robinson, chats with some of the children.

ENNISCORTHY REBELLION LEADERS, 1916. These were the leaders of the 1916 Rebellion in Enniscorthy. Back row: Una Brennan, Michael de Lacey, Eileen Hegarty. Front row: Seamus Rafter, Robert Brennan, Seamus Doyle and Sean Etchingham.

READY FOR ACTION, c. 1918. Uniformed members of the Connaught Rangers pose for this family photograph. Unfortunately their names are unknown.

SURRENDER, 1916. Enniscorthy was one of only two centres outside of Dublin that took part in the 1916 Rebellion. The headquarters for the Enniscorthy Volunteers was at the Athenaeum Hall in Castle Street. Enniscorthy surrendered on 1 May and the leaders and their company were led away to prison by British Army officers.

CHRISTMAS, 1916. Over 3,000 people were arrested in connection with the 1916 Rising and detained for varying periods, in various places. The majority were transported to Britain, although considerable numbers were released and allowed to return to Ireland after a short period of detention. Fifty-nine prisoners were removed from Richmond Barracks on 19 May and lodged in Lewes Detention Barracks on the following day. This group included a large number from Enniscorthy. The prisoners at Lewes were given an amnesty for Christmas Day, when this photograph was taken.

FREEDOM FIGHTERS, c. 1916. This group were involved in the War of Independence and some of them were involved in the Civil War. Back row: Donncadha O'Brien, Seamus Moran, Eamonn Murphy; front: Sean Moran (after whom Moran Park is named) and Thomas Doyle.

CUMANN Na mBAN, 1916. Another group, whose names have been lost. The photograph includes four women who would have been leading members of Cumann Na mBan and who did their patriotic duty at this tense and difficult time in the town's history.

VOLUNTEERS, 1916. St Patrick's Day and only a month to go before the Enniscorthy Easter Rising; members from Enniscorthy, Ferns and Wexford pose for the camera in Market Square. The man at the back is Tom Roche of Ferns, while fourth from the right in the back row is James Cullen and to his left, is Patrick Keegan.

RAFTER MONUMENT, 1958. Pictured at the unveiling of this monument to Seamus Rafter at Abbey Quay are the Trustees. The monument was moved to make way for changes to the Abbey Square in 1990, and the War of Independence patriot now faces eastwards across the river Slaney in the direction of Vinegar Hill. Included in the picture are T.J. Doyle, (chairman and treasurer), and P. Fitzpatrick (hon secretary).

SEAMUS RAFTER'S MEMORIAL, c. 1985. Commandant Seamus Rafter was one of the 1916 Volunteers in Enniscorthy. He died from injuries sustained in an explosion at The Cotton Tree, where he ran a provisions business, in September 1918. In 1958 this memorial was erected to his memory at Abbey Square.

RAFTER COMMEMORATION, 1950. Seamus Rafter was a native of Ballindaggin and he is buried in the local cemetery. There was a large turn out on this commemorative occasion.

PRESIDENTIAL VISIT, 1966.
President of Ireland, Eamon de
Valera (1959-1973) signs the
Distinguished Visitor's Book at the
Castle Museum while in Enniscorthy
for the centenary of the Mission
House. Noel Redmond shows the
President where to make his mark.
Senan Carty looks on from the back
of the group.

MAKE WAY FOR THE TAOISEACH, 1973. In the run-up to a general election, Taoiseach,
Jack Lynch pays a visit to the Fianna Fail cumann in Enniscorthy. He makes his way through
the crowd helped by Philip Acheson and Liam Kirwan.

OFF TO CHERNOBYL, 1996. Ambulances and aid were dispatched to Chernobyl on many occasions at around this time and the charity still continues. Enniscorthy played a major role in organising funds, and this photograph includes Andy and Joan Cloke, Cloheadon, who were the main fund-raisers and organisers, with the chief Ireland organiser, Adi Roche (white jumper, centre), who was a defeated candidate in the 1997 presidential election.

INTO EUROPE, 1974. It is Ireland's first day in the European Economic Community and Enniscorthy's UDC Chairman, Cllr James O'Leary, plants a tree at Parnell Road. Looking on are Mr O'Rourke, Donal Minnock (Town Clerk), Mr McGannon, Thomas Hayes, Jack Hayton and his three children, Eileen, Patricia and Liz Murphy, Michael Moore and John Daly.

Opposite: TWINNING WITH GIMONT, 1975. Enniscorthy became only the second town in Ireland to accept town twinning and on 3 April the official links were consolidated with the French town of Gimont. The Pact of Twinning was signed between Cllr Sean Sheahan, Chairman of Enniscorthy Urban District Council, and Monsieur Gabriel Dubarry, Mayor of Gimont.

TROUBLE ON THE RAILWAY, 1922. During the Civil War of 1922–23 the railway line between Enniscorthy and Wexford was regularly attacked and services were disrupted. This tactic was used to prevent troops being moved from the port of Rosslare. On this occasion the signal box at Enniscorthy has been ripped apart in an explosion. However, Inspector Forde and his gang are on hand to carry out speedy repairs and get services back to normal once more.

FULL STEAM UNDER THE TOWN, c. 1980. A once familiar scene is recreated by a special steam excursion run by the Railway Preservation Society of Ireland. Leaving Enniscorthy railway station the locomotive crosses the river Slaney before passing through the tunnel which takes it underneath the town centre. To the left is the spire of St Mary's church, dating from 1846, and to the right, The Maltings, where Wexford barley was converted into Guinness.

Four
Church and Education

MISSION FATHERS, 1946. Back row: Very Revd J. O'Doherty (Superior), Revd William higgins, Revd M. Doyle, Revd J. Devereux. Front row: Revd J. Flynn, Revd James Sinnott, .evd E.J. Ryan.

MISSION FATHERS, 1881. The central figure in the front row is Revd Abraham Brownrig then Superior of the Mission Fathers, made Bishop of Ossory in 1884. To his right is Fr Jame Cullen, founder of the Pioneer Total Abstinence Association, and second from right at th back is Fr Michael Kelly, who was consecrated Archbishop of Sydney in 1901.

THE MISSION HOUSE, c. 1915. After a few years in temporary accommodation th Missionaries of the Blessed Sacrament moved into the Mission House in about 1870. Richa Devereux of Wexford, who had made his fortune in the shipping trade, defrayed the expense the building on Shannon Hill which cost £1,200.

R JAMES CULLEN, c. 1912. Born at New Ross in 1841, the son of wealthy and charitable
rents, Fr Cullen spent fifteen years as a member of the House of Missions before joining the
suit Order in 1881. He is nationally known as the founder of the Pioneer Total Abstinence
ssociation. He died on 6 December 1921.

SHANNON CHURCH INTERIOR, c. 1915. This is a sight familiar to an older generation of worshippers at the Mission House; the first Mass was celebrated on Christmas Day 1866. The original seating capacity was for 350. This part of the church was retained, but significantly changed and incorporated into an extension when a new parish was created. The church was dedicated as St Senan's parish church in July 1975.

ST AIDAN'S CATHEDRAL, c. 1910. Built in 1846 to the design of the celebrated architect Augustus Welby Pugin, St Aidan's is the parish church at Enniscorthy and the seat of the Bishop of Ferns.

ST MARY'S CHURCH, *c.* 1900. Built in 1846 to serve the Church of Ireland community of the town and district, St Mary's was a replacement for an older church built on the same site but ruined as a consequence of the 1798 Rebellion. Located in the town centre it has posed many problems for photographers, even those with modern wide-lens equipment, but this shot taken from the rear of the building shows it to good effect, with the vestry door on the immediate right.

INTERIOR, ST MARY'S CHURCH, *c.* 1904.

EUCHARISTIC PROCESSION, c. 1910. Each year on the Feast of Corpus Christi the annual Eucharistic Procession of the Blessed Sacrament takes place. It starts from the Mission House and passes the New Range in the Shannon before making its way to Market Square and St Aidan's Cathedral on the other side of town.

EUCHARISTIC PROCESSION, c. 1944. Children wearing their First Holy Communion dresses lead the annual Corpus Christi Eucharistic Procession through Market Square. Townspeople erect bunting and hang out images of the Sacred Heart along the route of the procession which usually includes the bishop, local clergy and hundreds of lay people.

EUCHARISTIC PROCESSION, 1990. Revd Denis Brennan, Administrator, St Senan's Parish, blesses the altar in Market Square while the Bishop of Ferns, the Most Revd Brendan Comiskey, (left foreground) kneels in silent prayer.

LORETO CONVENT, 1946. This house was built in 1798 and was originally the bishop's residence; however, the facade seen here was the result of renovation and expansion in 1939. The Loreto nuns came to town and established a school here in 1872. The house next door was acquired by them in 1878, and is now Dr Cuddigan's Nursing Home. The Loreto Convent School, which turned out many distinguished students, closed its doors in 1969.

ORCHESTRA TIME, c. 1920. Learning musical skills at the Loreto Convent.

COOKING CLASS, *c.* 1920. The students learn the skills of good cooking at the Loreto Convent. The Sacred Heart looks down upon them in spiritual guidance. The convent was opened in 1872 and this kitchen was added in 1900.

GUIDES AND BROWNIES, *c.* 1965. The Enniscorthy Guide Company and Brownie Pack with leaders and the rector, Canon N.D. Bowers. The leaders are Joan Deacon, Edith Kearon, Dorothy Cookman, Iris Browne and Canon Bowers.

SCOUTS, 1973. The local Scout movement had no shortage of recruits and enthusiastic members. We could be forgiven for thinking that they were females, but long hair was the fashion in those days.

IRISH LANGUAGE PROMOTION GROUP, 1902. Promoting the Irish language in Enniscorthy were, front row, left to right: Paddy Byrne, Revd Sean Dunne, Michael O'Sullivan Revd Patrick Murphy, Andrew Furlong, P.F. Keenan. Back row: T. O'Cnaimin, William Stamp, Revd William Harper, Henry Dillon, Revd Robert Fitzhenry, Thomas O'Cathain Joseph Sinnott, Liam Mac Giolla Craoibhe.

THE CATHEDRAL CHOIR, 1946. Front row: Miss Mary O'Kelly, Mrs M. Walsh, Mr Henry J. Roche, Miss Kathleen Grattan-Flood (N.T.), Mrs H.J. Roche, Miss J. O'Kelly. Second row: Miss Doris Greene, Miss A. O'Leary, Mrs M.J. Kavanagh, Miss M. Leacy, Miss Josephine Roche, Mrs Hasslacher, Miss M. Grattan-Flood (N.T.), Miss Emily Nolan. Third row: Miss M. Codd, Miss C. Lambert, Miss N. Walsh, Mrs A. Martin, Miss Lucking, Miss B. Ringwood, Miss R. Murphy, Miss N. Hanlon. Back row: Liam Devereux, William Moore, Martin Kirwan, Tom Askins, Michael Hanlon, P. Askins, T. Murphy, James Ringwood.

ENNISCORTHY C.B.S. PLAIN CHANT, 1960. Back row: Jim Farrell (Clonhaston), Nicky Tyrrell, Jimmy Waddick (Ross Road), Matt Gahan (Esmonde Road), Billy Hudson (Irish Street), Aidan Wildes (The Shannon), Tony Courtney (Ross Road). Third row: Michael Hyland (Bellefield), Neil Carty (Bellefield), Eamon Carty, Sean O'Donoghue (Bellefield), Declan O'Connor (Slaney Street), Liam Doyle (Bellefield). Second row: Martin Bracken, Michael Murphy (Pearse Road, brother of Sean in front row), Tom Kearney (Patrick's Place), John Canavan, Harry O'Connor (Hospital Lane), Christy Doyle (St Aidan's Villas), Tom Furlong. Front row: Peter Murphy (Upper Weafer Street), Michael Foley (Munster Hill), Michael Lynch (Rafter Street), Billy Martin (Hempfield), Sean Murphy and Seamus Hogan (John Street).

ST MARY'S NEW SCHOOL, 1951. Happy pupils line up for the photographer at the opening of a new two-teacher school for the Church of Ireland community. In the picture is Mr Jack Hayton, who was the principal from 1936 until 1976, and Miss K.E. Patton, who served with him for over twenty years, was then appointed to succeed him and held the post until her retirement in 1984.

Opposite: ST MARY'S NATIONAL SCHOOL, SENIOR CLASS, c. 1950. Back row: Tom Smith, Leslie Doherty, Edelyn Crofts, Jacqueline Doherty, Tom Crofts, Ann Wilkie, Walter Doherty, Adrian Empey. Middle row: Lillian Wheelock, Fred Earle, -?-, -?- , Daphne Wheelock, Eleanor Borthistle. Front row: Henry Dale, Ken Marshall, Noel Hayden, John Murphy, Adrian Youell, John Sheil.

ST MARY'S NATIONAL SCHOOL, JUNIOR CLASS, c. 1950. Back row: Joe Smith, Edith Sheil, Clive Allen, Margaret Doherty, Gerald James, Gethyn Leech, Teddy Plummer, Elan Armstrong, Jennifer Armstrong, Douglas Armstrong. Third row: Alan Doherty, Helen Rothwell, Primrose Wheelock, Victor Martin, Valerie Sutton, Micheal Empey, Avis Marshall, Ronnie Earle, Eleanor Borthistle. Second row: Edna Sheil, Janet McGill, Jean Doherty, Hilda Sheil, Victor Ruttle, Gerald James, Eric Levingstone, Helen Youell, Diane Armstrong. Front row: George Leech, Linda Hatton, ? Youell, Kathleen Hatton, Kenneth Leech, Jane Warren, David McGill, Olive Dale.

PRESBYTERIAN CHURCH, 1985. The United Presbyterian and Methodist church at Mill Park Road has served the Presbyterian community since 1866. A year later, Revd William Arnold, who is commemorated in Arnold's Cross, was ordained in the church and lived to minister to those under his charge for almost forty-eight years.

REVEREND JOSEPH RANSON, c. 1965. The founder of the County Museum at Enniscorthy, this Kilmuckridge-born priest was deeply interested in history, especially local history, and also archaeology and folklore. When Enniscorthy Castle was offered for sale in 1961, Fr Ranson persuaded the governing body of the Athenaeum Hall to purchase the building and convert it into a folk museum. The museum has become one of Co. Wexford's best known tourist attractions and has been visited by people from all over the world. Father Ranson died in 1964.

DIAMOND JUBILEE, 1931. Survivors of the Men's Confraternity at Enniscorthy, who joined up in 1871, assembled for their diamond jubilee celebrations and posed for the photographer. Front row: Thomas Murphy, James Mythen, Brian Kearns, John Forrestal, Thomas Keegan, Joseph Barker, John Carroll, Thomas O'Rourke, Patrick O'Reilly, James Doyle. Back row: Timothy Butler, Patrick Bernie, John Kenny, Richard Roche, Philip Hendrick, John Devereux, Thomas O'Leary, Mogue Murphy.

WOMEN'S JUBILARIANS, 1946. These women enrolled in the St Aidan's Parish Confraternity in 1871 and retained unbroken membership until this photograph was taken sixty years later. Front row: Mrs M. Delaney, Miss A. Hanley, Mrs Sarah Sheridan, Mrs Elizabeth O'Neill, Mrs Bridget Howell, Mrs A. Murphy, Mrs Devereux, Mrs K. Redmond, Mrs H. Francis, Mrs Bridget Murphy. Back row: Mrs Mary Byrne, Mrs Catherine Leacy, Mrs Mary Murphy, Mrs O'Leary, Mrs S. Hendrick, Mrs Mary Keegan, Mrs Kearns, Mrs C. Morrissey, Mrs W. Doyle, Mrs Mary Kirwan, Mrs A.M. Mitten, Miss B. Doran, Mrs Ellen Pierce, Mrs Mary Foley, Miss K. Corcoran.

HOLY FAMILY CONFRATERNITY BAND, 1945. Back row: William Moore, J. Dempsey, W. Davis, G. Doherty, S. O'Dowd, R. Davis, M. Kinnaird. Middle row: B. Dempsey, D. Murphy, J. Ruth, W. O'Hanlon, Tom Askins, Christy O'Toole, M. O'Hanlon. Front row: P. Murphy, W. Martin, Eddie Askins, Willie O'Connor, Revd P.J. Murphy, Revd J. Codd (Adm. St Aidan's Parish), J. Walsh, Revd P. Quaid, Revd J. Ranson, J. Boyne, T. Leacy.

Five
Social and Leisure

CLONHASTON GARDEN PARTY, 1982. Parents and children from the Clonhaston district were treated to a summer fete. These included, back row: Bernadette Doyle with baby Graham, Anne Martin, Mary Hughes, Helen Martin, Patty and Mary Redmond, Laura Doyle, Joanie Ormonde. Middle row: Mary and Kathleen Doyle, Lorraine Ormonde, Emma and Mairead Redmond, Linda Fitzpatrick. Front row: Nicola Martin, Claire Redmond, Sinead Doyle, Nollaig Martin, John Ormonde, Michael and Shane Martin. Kneeling in front: Pauline Redmond and Donna Fitzpatrick.

EDERMINE HOUSE, c. 1898. Lady Power entertains friends, including Philip Alcock of Wilton Castle, in the beautiful grounds of her country house at Edermine. The magnificent early Victorian iron conservatory in the background was designed by Richard Turner and erected by James Pierce of Wexford.

TAKING AIM, 1978. Field Day fun at St Senan's; Michael Murphy (Esmonde Road), aims for the top prize in the rifle shoot.

RETIREMENT, 1977. Pat Dempsey retired from the staff of the Co-op and fellow worker Michael Doyle was on hand to present the wallet of notes on behalf of all those who contributed to the collection. His wife, Elizabeth also enjoyed the night out.

NICK'S RETIREMENT, 1977. Nick Hogan (Slaney View Park), third from the left, is pictured with his wife, Kit, on the occasion of his retirement from the staff of J. Donohoe Ltd. The celebrating couple are flanked by Nick's working colleagues, John Kehoe and Phil Reilly.

OPENING THE STRAWBERRY FAIR, *c.* 1974. Famous television personality Eamonn Andrews opens the Strawberry Fair before a capacity crowd in Abbey Square. Looking on at the bandstand are locals Johnny O'Leary, Davy Murphy and Jimmy Owens.

HOSPITAL DINNER DANCE, 1974. Enjoying themselves at the St John's hospital dinner dance were staff members Eilish Hughes (nee Booth), Margo Leacy, and Liz Connick.

FERNS CHARITY WALKERS, 1973. Mairead Doyle (kneeling) leads the Cheshire Walk from Ferns to Enniscorthy, helped out by Misses O'Leary, Foley, -?- and Cowman.

THE FRENCH CIRCLE, c. 1975. Through the efforts of Madame Duffy (*Chantemonde*, Weafer Street), Enniscorthy French Circle was set up. This was one of their well attended meetings with Mr Franklin in the foreground, backed up by a happy group of local nuns.

SIGNING BOOKS, 1983. At the launch of this author's book, *Family Industry in Enniscorthy*, in the summer of 1983, are Cllr Sean Sheahan, Chairman of Enniscorthy Urban District Council, Dan Walsh, Tom Davis of S. & A.G. Davis Ltd, Margaret Walsh, Nick Mernagh, Chairman of the County Museum and local businessman, Myles Kehoe.

RELAXING FARMERS, 1974. These members of the farming community have seen it all. It is time for relaxation and a chat about times gone by.

THE SOCIAL SCENE, 1980. Maureen and Seamus Moynihan, and Patricia and Aidan Wildes enjoy the annual dinner dance at H. Murphy & Co. It was popular for local firms to hold staff social events every year, usually around Christmas.

CAIM F.C.A. GROUP, c. 1975. Pictured at the annual social and presentation of awards are the members of Caim F.C.A. Back row: Martin Asple, Jim Dunne, Jim Byrne, Hugh Dunne, John Howlin, ? Buckley, Dessie Furlong, Billy Buckley, Joe Kehoe. Front row: Pat Foley, Revd Tom Doyle C.C. (Courtnacuddy), Bobby Reck, Joe Quigley, Revd Harry Sinnott, C.C. (Caim), Pat Hennessy, and Revd Patrick Furlong, C.C. (Kiltealy).

ABBEY PICTURE HOUSE, 1914. This was the town's first cinema, located in Abbey Square. This group of workers shares a few quiet moments with Thomas McCarthy, the proprietor, fourth from the right. The others are, from left to right: William Kelly, Jim Newman, Bernard Murray, Ms Coughlan, Mr Vaughan, Matty O'Neill and Peter Sinnott. Mr McCarthy was twice Chairman of Enniscorthy Urban Council, from 1920 until 1934 and from 1945 until 1947.

O'NEILL FAMILY REUNION, 1992. Emigration took its toll on local families over the years and still continues to be a factor in family life. Here we have a good example of a family reunion for the O'Neills. Front: Molly Murphy (Warwickshire), Kathleen Wickham (Manchester), Peggy Martin and Breda Howarth (both in London), Lily Dobmeir (United States) and Mary Millar (London). At the back are Barney O'Neill (London) and P.J. O'Neill (Pearse Road, Enniscorthy).

ECHO STAFF, 1979 (opposite). In July, machine minder Eddie Busher decided to give up the day job and make his fortune in Australia. His colleagues turned out to wish him a *bon voyage* in Newe's of Templeshannon. Back row: Jimmy Gahan, John Roche, Tom Colgan, Padge Murphy, Eddie Tobin, Dan Hudson, Marie Mackey. Middle row: Sean Whelan, Michael Murphy, Tommy Clifford. Front row: Michael Whelan, James 'Dickie' Quirke, Gloria Sinnott (who made the presentation), Eddie Busher, Ned Fenlon, Matty Cloke, Danny Kennedy and Brian Hogan.

THE FIRST PICTURE SHOW, c. 1955. It's Christmas and the boys of Enniscorthy enjoy a picture show in the Boy's Club.

WEXFORD SCOUTS, 1928. This group paid a visit to Enniscorthy and showed off some of their skills in Whelan's yard on Island Road.

ART MacMURROUGH'S WAR PIPE BAND, *c.* 1920. This is a fine photograph but unfortunately all records of the band's activities and their names appear to be lost.

IRISH NATIONAL FORESTERS' BRASS AND REED BAND, 1917. Pictured outside the Foresters' Rooms in Court Street are, back row: L.J. Lynch, T. Driscoll, D. O'Farrell, F. Murphy, M. Sullivan, E. Somers, J.McCarthy, J. Gerathy, P. Dunne. Front row: M. Maguire, T. Coghlan, J. Wickham, P. Murphy, D. O'Connor, M. Somers, J. Moran and, seated, J.J. Somers and J. Coghlan.

Six

Sport

THE TROPHY HAUL, 1968. It is the end of the season and members of St Patrick's Boxing Club pose for the photographer with their impressive trophy collection. Back row, left to right: Noel Farrell, Mick Quigley (trainer), Dalton Ronan, Toddy Brogan, Andrew Hutchinson, Harry O'Connor, Mick Murphy, Mossy Rigley, Bernard Dunne, John McCarthy (club chairman), Larry Canavan. Front row: Mick Healy, -?-, ? Brogan, Aidan Murphy, Mick Millar, Dicky Murphy, Christy O'Connor and Michael Cogley.

MICK QUIGLEY, 1959. This Greenville man has devoted a lifetime to boxing. In his young days he was one of the champions of the ring in the colours of Arklow and Boolavogue Boxing Clubs. He is still very much involved in the sport and is a referee, qualified to international standards. He has also been trainer to Boolavogue Boxing Club and St Patrick's Boxing Club in Enniscorthy.

ST PATRICK'S BOXING CLUB, 1978. Nostalgia from the scrapbook for the founding members of St Patrick's Boxing Club on the occasion of their silver jubilee celebrations in November. From left to right: Joe Cash (former trainer), Bill Barry (well known dentist and founder member), Mick Quigley (trainer) and Seosamh O'Cuinneagain (well known solicitor and founder member).

ALL IRELAND CHAMPIONS, 1974. Shown here are some of the greatest boxers Enniscorthy has ever produced and winners of numerous All Ireland boxing titles. From St Patrick's Boxing Club are John McCarthy (chairman), Jim O'Sullivan, who won ten National Senior titles, Mick Millar, Gus Farrell and Bernard Dunne (trainer).

BOY'S CLUB, 1956. This group of young hopefuls were members of the Enniscorthy Boy's Club boxing team who took on Wicklow in November of that year. The back row includes Bill Barry Joseph Cunningham, Mick Quinn (with towel around neck), Fr Tony Scallan and Peeny Led on the extreme right.

STAR ATHLETE, 1974. Champion track and field athlete, Mary Treacy, whose father hailed from Enniscorthy, paid a visit to the town for a coaching session. She took time out to sign autographs for the junior members of Enniscorthy Athletic Club.

NISSAN CLASSIC, 1986. Some of the best cyclists in the world, including the Irish pair, Stephen Roche (winner of the Tour de France) and Sean Kelly, competed in the Nissan Classic which passed through Enniscorthy. They tested the new road surface at Brownswood which had been widened and aligned the previous year.

BORRMOUNT HORSESHOE TEAM, 1980. Horseshoe pitching enjoyed a popular run at the end of the 1970s and into the 1980s. One of the most successful teams in the country hailed from Borrmount. Pictured here with an impressive haul of trophies are P.J. Merriman, Paddy Walsh, Mick Kirwan, Johnny O'Leary, Paddy O'Leary, Peter Kehoe, Paddy Long and Joe O'Leary.

DORAN'S BRIDGE, c. 1975. Keen rivals to Borrmount on many occasions and champions too, this team came from the Ferns area and were experts in the sport of horseshoe pitching. Back row: Charlie Christopher, Bill Maher, Owen Levingstone, Paddy Byrne. Front row: Tommy Carter, Bill Byrne, Jim Byrne, Jack Sharpe.

HUNTING ON BREE HILL, c. 1910. Wexford has a proud tradition of hunting and the Bree district has always been good for the sport, with lots of coverts and double bans. Major Charlie Beatty was one of the best Masters to put the hounds through their paces.

COUNTING THE HOUNDS, c. 1910. Foxhunting has always been a feature of rural life in Co. Wexford. The Island Foxhounds and the Bree Foxhounds hunt respectively east and west of the river Slaney.

OTTER HOUNDS, 1899. The Kendal Otter hounds paid a visit to Ireland in the summer of 1899. One port of call was Wilton Castle, where they were greeted by the landlord, Philip Alcock, seen in the centre with a cloth cap and a gun over his shoulder.

ENNISCORTHY JUDO TEAM, 1969. A judo team existed in the town for about fifteen years, but sadly, this martial arts discipline is no longer practised in Enniscorthy. Back row: John Leacy, Larry Byrne, Jim Murphy, Christy Doyle. Front row: Tony Moorehouse, Eamonn Casey and Seamus O'Brien.

ENNISCORTHY PIGEON CLUB, 1968. Collecting trophies for their prize-winning birds are from left to right: Harry and Tony Bolger, Tom Millar, Aidan Whelan, James O'Connor, Tom Quinn and John Dobbs.

CATS GAME, 1975. This unusual street game was once very popular in Enniscorthy. In this scene on the Fairgreen, Lar Rigley is about to strike the ball. The game was described as a combination of rounders and cricket and an object like a starting handle was used to strike the ball, which was manufactured from timber. Local lore says that the game was brought to the town from Wales by the Owens family.

CYCLE OUTING, 1974. This group is ready to set off from Abbey Square on a leisurely cycle ride. Some of them went on to join Enniscorthy Cycling Club, sharing in its many successes and enjoyment.

ENNISCORTHY ATHLETIC CLUB, 1975. This group, complete with new track suits, reflects the strength of juvenile athletics in the town at this time. Many of them achieved great success in both track, field and cross country championships at all levels.

GOLDFINCH SINGERS, 1974. Enniscorthy was unique in the fact that it once had a cage bird society. They used to hold singing competitions for birds which were hugely competitive and keenly contested, even if the rules caused occasional problems! This enthusiastic group were competing in a section confined to goldfinches. At the back are: Tom Murphy, Josie Flood, Laurence Murphy, Paddy O'Connor, Joe Rigley, Paddy Murphy, Michael O'Connor, Laurence Sinnott, Bob Peare and John Carroll. In the front: Peter O'Brien, Pat Flood, Phelim O'Connor and Martin Collins. Who are the boys at the front?

PITCH 'N' PUTT WINNERS, 1974. The presentation of the Kavanagh Cup following a successful Pitch 'n' Putt competition in St Patrick's Park. The group includes Seamus Boyne, Seamus Comerford, Liam Kenny, Danny Murphy, Tom Brennan, Peter Carroll, Pat Jordan, William Doyle and Aidan Murphy.

BOATING ENTHUSIASTS, 1974. It is prize giving time for the canoeists of Slaney Boat Club. The names of the juveniles are forgotten but the adults include Jim Ringwood, Jim Quinn, James Symes, the manager of the Bank of Ireland, who presented some of the trophies, and Tony Murphy.

ENNISCORTHY COURSING CLUB, 1975. The town has had a coursing club for many years and ran an annual meeting in the showgrounds. At the back are: John Carty, Paddy Griffin, Sean Carty, Tom Hatton, Eugene Crosbie, John Doran, -?-, -?-. In the front are: Willie Cullen, Gerry Carty, Simon Kavanagh, Maureen Tobin, Eddie Tobin and Harry Larkin.

HANDBALL CHAMPIONS, c. 1975. Members of Enniscorthy Handball Club collect their trophies following their success at Bellefield Shown; here are Patrick Nolan, Jackser Owens later a member of Enniscorthy UDC, Michael Collins, Noel Goff and Michael Whelan.

FERNS ATHLETIC CLUB, *c.* 1973. Celebrating twenty five years of Ferns Athletic Club are, back row: Michael Murphy (jnr), Kevin Killeen, Mick Kenny, Pat O'Neill, -?-, Michael Nolan, Luke Kehoe, Jim Kearney, Barty Kehoe, Joe Jackman, Billy Harpur. Front row: -?-, Aidan Murphy, Very Revd Fr Gahan, Michael Murphy (chairman), Helen Banville, Dan Walsh (P.R.O., County BLE Board).

FERNS G.A.A. CLUB, *c.* 1974. This group of Ferns G.A.A. stalwarts from the 1950s got together for a memorable reunion in Enniscorthy. Reminiscing about memorable days on the hurling pitch are, back row: Toddy Holden, Michael O'Neill, Mick Byrne, John Nolan, Johnny Foley, Pat Maguire, Eamonn Kiely, Pat Furlong. Third row: Paddy Murphy, Joe Bolger, Johnny Fortune, Pa Plummer, Kevin Quigley, Shay O'Neill, Aidan Plummer, Jim Maher. Second row: Aidan Murphy, Sgt Reynolds, Dick Nolan, Michael Sinnott, Joe O'Neill, John Dempsey. Front row: Jim Byrne, Colm O'Neill, Seamus Redmond, Tom Furlong and Mylie Breen

TALKING HURLING, 1996 (above left). All Ireland senior hurling championship medal holder (with Wexford, 1968) and local businessman, Phil Wilson of Siopa Brog, Castle Street, examines the hurley of a legend, Mick Mackey of Limerick. With him is an interested John Kenny, caretaker at the Athenaeum Hall. THE BOB O'KEEFFE CUP, 1970 (above right). Michael Collins (Moran Park), captain of the Wexford senior hurling team, raises the Leinster trophy following his team's success.

ST AIDAN'S HURLING CLUB, 1962. This team was Special Junior Championship winners. Back row: Benny Maguire (selector), Tom Maher, Michael Furlong (sub), S. O'Leary, N. Walsh, D. McCoy, B. Quirke, P. Kirwan, J. Browne (sub), P. Fitzpatrick, Michael Hernan (sub) and Liam Browne (sub). Front row: Martin Doyle (trainer and selector), Joe Morrissey, Joe Doyle, Jim Balfe (sub), Michael Roban, John O'Neill, Jim Brady, Billy Davis, Billy O'Toole, Jim Quirke.

P.H. PEARSES' HURLING CLUB, 1945. On 31 October 1945, this team from Enniscorthy defeated St Vincent's (Dublin) in the curtain-raiser to the Oireachtais Final between Galway and Tipperary at Croke Park. Back row: John Quinn (sub.), Ted Bolger (capt.), Harry Larkin, Art Foley, Tom Balfe (sub.), George Pepper, Noel Quigley, Jack Walsh, Bob Slater, Sammy Walsh, Martin Carroll. Front row: Senan Dwyer, John Treacy (sub.), Michael Leacy, Felix Murphy, Liam Byrne, Pat Leacy, Ger Newe, Dai Tobin, Martin Doyle (selector), and Tom Dixon.

ROGER CASEMENT'S HURLING CLUB, 1959. Emigrants to Britain fostered hurling and many of the locals who saw the game for the first time were amazed at its speed and skill. This team, based in Coventry, won the league and championship in 1959, '64 and '70, and for good measure also won the football league in 1964. Back row: Mick O'Brien (Tipperary), selector, Micheal Hogan (Kilkenny), Mick and Maurice Goggins (Wexford), John Malone (Tipperary), Bill, Pat and Martin Murphy (Marshalstown, Enniscorthy), Charlie Crowe (Ballygarrett, Co. Wexford), Kevin Cardiff (Wicklow), selector. Front row: John Maher (Kilkenny), Mick Feeney (Galway), Brendan Weir (Westmeath), Michael Jordan (Tomahurra, Enniscorthy), Danny Coady (Dublin), Padraig Stephens (Roscommon), P.J. Ronan (Kilkenny).

MYLES KEHOE'S TEAM, *c.* 1975. During the 1970s many business premises and industrial firms participated in an 11-a-side football tournament run in conjunction with the annual Strawberry Fair. It was always great fun and one of the highlights of past fairs. Myles Kehoe's team consisted of, back row: Jim Quirke, Matty Reddy, Tom Peare, Paddy Nolan and Sean Doyle. Front row: Martin Hall, Ned Fenlon, Joe Morrissey, Eddie Kehoe (captain), Michael O'Leary and Benny Sullivan.

MINOR HURLING CHAMPIONS, 1909. The Red Rapparees were a famous and much-feared hurling team from Enniscorthy. They achieved championship success at a minor level and many of the young players were destined to win further honours in later years. Back row: W. Banim, E. Duff, P. Breen, J. Ryan, L. Gahan. Middle row: F. Murphy, T. O'Leary, J. Sinnott, P. Doran, J. Dempsey. Front row: F. Grady, V. Connolly, T. Hayes, P. Smyth (captain), J. Gahan D. Murphy, R. O'Leary.

JUVENILE CHAMPIONS, 1974. Seen here are members of the Starlights Football Club, who were the County Juvenile Champions. Back row, left to right: Paddy Murphy, Edward Doran, Martin Kehoe, Joe Newe, Dan Jordan, Tommy Tyrrell, Billy Reid, Mick Sullivan, John O'Rourke. Front row: Peter O'Brien, Noel Kenny, James O'Sullivan, Padraig Doyle, Frankie Farnan, Patrick Doyle, Nicky Murphy.

ENNISCORTHY TOWN AFC, 1978. Back row, left to right: Michael Kearney, ? Butler, John Freeman, Jimmy Morrissey, Paddy Nolan, Charlie O'Brien (manager). Front row: P.J. Fortune, Paddy Murphy, Matty Butler, Danny O'Rourke, Martin Whelan and Billy Reid.

ENNISCORTHY UNITED AFC, 1978. Back row, left to right: Dan Jordan, Billy Hudson, Tommy Hutchinson, P.J. Murphy, Ned Carthy, Tom Wildes, Sean Nolan. Front row: Tony Kenny, Michael Millar, Vinnie O'Sullivan, Paddy O'Connor and Michael Larkin.

JIM BYRNE CUP WINNERS, 1977. Success for the Enniscorthy Starlights in the Jim Byrne Cup football competition. Back row, left to right: James O'Sullivan, Michael O'Leary, Edward Doran, Joe Newe, Paddy Murphy, Billy Morrissey, Tommy Tyrrell, Pat Creane. Front row: Patrick Doyle, Nicky Murphy, Peter O'Brien, Frankie Farnan, Jim Rigley, Warren Doyle, Padraig Doyle, Dan Jordan.

Seven
Personalities and Places

FUNERAL OF SENATOR JOHN O'LEARY, 1959. Members of the Labour Party, led by Bob Peare (left) and Willie Carley (right), head a guard of honour beside the hearse carrying the coffin of Senator John O'Leary, 1894–1959, as it travelled along Irish Street on its way to St Mary's Cemetery. Mr O'Leary, who was a member of Enniscorthy Urban District Council for a quarter of a century, represented his native town in Dail, Eireann, between 1943 and 1957. He was a member of Seanad Eireann at the time of his death. The Dodge hearse belonged to O'Reillys, a local firm of undertakers.

WILLIAM FORTUNE, *c*. 1906. Proprietor of the steam saw mills (recently vacated by Wexford County Council) and a well known builder and contractor at Lower Church Street, William Fortune was a man of tremendous business acumen which was reflected in the success of everything he attempted. In 1905, he obtained a certificate of merit at the County Wexford Feis Industrial Exhibition in New Ross. Amongst the local buildings attributed to his building firm are Enniscorthy Post Office, the Provincial Bank (now the Allied Irish Bank, Slaney Place), the Convent at Bunclody, Brownswood House for Baroness Gray and additions to St Senan's Hospital. He also built the dispensary and residence at Clonroche and undertook alterations to Bolger & Co., at George Street (now Rafter Street). He once employed eighty tradesman at his premises on the lower end of Abbey Quay.

BROWNSWOOD HOUSE, 1902. Brownswood, a red-bricked English manor house, was designed by Thomas Drew and completed in 1896 at a cost of £4,000. It was built for Baroness Gray by Enniscorthy building contractor William Fortune.

THE CAREWS, 1914. Lord and Lady
Carew of Castleboro House take a stroll
in the grounds of their magnificent
mansion. As landlords they were
admired in the local community.

LADY CAREW, 1899. This historic
photograph was taken on the occasion of
Lady Carew's 100th birthday. She also
achieved the unique distinction of
having lived in three different centuries;
she was born in 1799 and died in 1901.
She was born Jane Catherine Cliffe of
Bellevue, Co. Wexford, and was the wife
of the first Lord Carew of Castleboro.

CASTLEBORO BOUND, *c.* 1910. This winter scene shows a white horse and trap on the avenue leading to Castleboro House.

CASTLEBORO HOUSE, *c.* 1890. The home of the Carew family, this was a magnificent classical house, designed by Daniel Robertson, consisting of a three storey central block of 90 ft flanked by two wings, each of 55 ft. By the time it was completed in 1858 it had cost £84,000.

CASTLEBORO HOUSE, *c.* 1890. Many people erroneously imagine that this should be the front of Castleboro House, and who can blame them? This extraordinary lofty portico is supported by six Corinthian columns. Burned in the Civil War of 1923, the ruins of Castleboro remain one of the most popular architectural attractions in Co. Wexford today.

CASTLEBORO LIBRARY, *c.* 1890. This view shows just one aspect of the beautiful interior of the mansion; note the stunning marble sculptured figures.

ROLAND RICHARDS, 1930. The Richards family lived at Solsborough House between 1688 and the death of this man, the last owner of the estate, who died in March 1935 at the ripe old age of 82.

FIRE AT SOLSBOROUGH, 1933. The house was accidentally razed to a ruin in a midday fire on 19 April. It is believed that the fire originated in snowboards and other timber placed on the roof.

SOLSBOROUGH HOUSE, *c.* 1920. This was probably an early nineteenth century house that was built as an enlargement for an older one. It was from Solsborough that General Lake led his army in its attack against the insurgents on Vinegar Hill on 21 June 1798.

MAYFIELD HOUSE, *c.* 1930. Located in the town centre off Lymington Road, it is the former home of the O'Flaherty family, who were well known solicitors. It is now the home of John and Marian Roche.

COMMANDER DAVID BEATTY, 1898. Born in 1871, David Beatty joined the Navy in 1884 and fourteen years later, when this photograph was taken, he was promoted to the rank of commander. By 1916 he was Vice-Admiral of the Fleet and was involved in the Battle of Jutland in the North Sea and the Battle of Scapa Flow, off the Scottish coast. In 1919 he became the youngest admiral since Nelson and the King conferred on him the titles, Baron Beatty of the North Sea and Brooksby in the County of Leicester, Viscount Borodale of Wexford, and Earl Beatty. He died in 1936 and is buried in St Paul's Cathedral, London.

YOUNG BEATTY, *c.* 1881. Even at a very early age, the young David Beatty was thinking of a career at sea. He grew up at Borodale and was destined to rule the waves.

MAJOR CHARLES BEATTY, *c.* 1914. Brother of Admiral Beatty of Borodale, Charles served in South Africa as ADC to the Brigadier General of the Mounted Infantry Brigade, and during the campaign was twice mentioned in dispatches, awarded the Queen's Medal with six clasps and the DSO. At the outbreak of the First World War he offered his services; in 1916 he was badly wounded at Flanders and had to have an arm amputated. In the summer of that year he returned to his home at Borodale, but was in poor health and died aged 47, in March 1917. He was an accomplished horseman and finished second in the Aintree Grand National of 1897 on *Filbert.* He also trained the winner of the 1905 Ascot Cup.

LADY POWER, *c*. 1898. The well dressed footman prepares the horse and trap for Lady Power of Edermine House before she set out on the short journey to Enniscorthy.

Edermine.

EDERMINE HOUSE, *c*. 1940. Formerly the seat of the O'Toole family, it was home to Sir John Power and other members of the family – the Powers of whiskey distilling fame – from 1835 until the 1950s. The architect of the house was John B. Keane, who died in 1859. At the time of this photograph, it was the residence of Miss Jane Ryan. She promoted crafts and customs for the benefit of the Irish Countrywomen's Association.

THE ALCOCK GIRLS, *c.* 1923. The four daughters of Philip and Mrs Alcock of Wilton Castle: Kathleen Alcock, Philippa Curtis, Mary Galloway and Margaret Parshall.

WILTON CASTLE, *c.* 1890. Although dating from the thirteenth century, the modern appearance of Wilton Castle (although in ruins since 1923) is attributed to the liaison between landlord, Harry Alcock, and his architect, Daniel Robertson, who carried out extensive restoration work in the period 1841–1844. It is now the property of Sean Windsor, whose generosity and support over the years is much appreciated.

WILTON CASTLE. Co. WEXFORD. 2033. WIL.

GENIUS OF THE WIRELESS, *c.* 1884. The inventor of wireless, Guglielmo Marconi, was the son of an Enniscorthy woman, Annie Jameson of The Still. His maternal family gained fame in the whiskey trade, while he pioneered wireless and radio.

P.J. ROCHE, *c.* 1900. From moderate beginnings, he became a businessman in New Ross and Enniscorthy from about 1853, although his Enniscorthy concern only really got going with the purchase of Morans grain business. He established The Maltings at Enniscorthy, but also purchased the castle which was in ruins, and after major restoration his son lived there. Had it not been for him, Enniscorthy's twelfth century castle would now be a ruin instead of a fine County Museum. He died in 1905, but his family were later connected through marriage with President Kennedy's family.

WALTER SINNOTT, *c.* 1890. This enterprising man from Glenbrien bought a wine, beer and whiskey bonding business, previously operated by Strangman-Davis at No. 7 Castle Hill, in 1852. He also sold groceries and died a bachelor, leaving the business to his niece, Mary Sinnott.

MARY SINNOTT, *c.* 1915. The great-grandmother of Harry Kehoe, the fifth generation to trade at Castle Hill. Mary inherited the grocery and bar business at Castle Hill from her uncle, Water Sinnott, and traded successfully along with her husband, James, until 1921. She was a member of an old Enniscorthy family, 'Byrne's of the Chapel', and died in 1927.

MRS HAROLD LETT, c. 1910. This English lady married into the Beatty family of Borodale and, frustrated by the poor quality of life endured by women, she decided in 1910, along with some friends, to established the United Irishwomen. The name was later changed to the Irish Countrywomen's Association, which is now the largest women's organisation in the country. After her husband's death she married local farmer and businessman, Harold Lett. Mrs Lett died in 1940 and is buried in Clonmore Churchyard.

BREE HALL, 1970. This modest, galvanised hall was built by local contractor Martin Doyle assisted by Nicholas Flood, in 1911. It served the community of Bree, just six miles from Enniscorthy. It was associated with the early days of the Irish Countrywomen's Association which was founded in 1910. Typical of rural halls of its time, it played host to concerts and other entertainments in a bygone era. It has long since been demolished and is now the site of the I.C.A. Commemoration Garden.

SADIE SOMERS, 1980. The longest serving member in the history of the Irish Countrywomen's Association, she was named ICA Award Winner and is seen here at the sundial in Bree, which marks the foundation in June 1910 of the largest women's movement in Ireland.

SAM BRICKLEY, c, 1915. This man inherited the art of pottery manufacturing and continued to work every day until he was 87 years old. He had a good retirement too. He lived to the rip old age of 105, and his wife, Mary lived to be 101. They had six children and sixty two grandchildren and great-grandchildren.

MR HERBERT MURPHY (1895-1981) *c.* 1930. The founder of the wholesale firm H. Murphy & Company, now one of the biggest Cash and Carry outfits in the south-east, with a branch in Arklow since 1969. Mr Murphy succeeded his father in 1921 as a representative at the old established firm of A.S. Davis Ltd in Mill Park Road. As a young man he was an accomplished sportsman in hockey, cricket and rugby.

THE LAST TEA BLENDER, 1980. Sean Sheahan was a tea blender and chief taster at the firm of H. Murphy & Co., and was the last of his trade in Enniscorthy. On his retirement the company ceased to produce 'loose' tea, which was being challenged by the growing popularity of tea-bags, marketed by firms of national and international repute. Mr Sheahan was a public representative for many years and served as Chairman of Enniscorthy Urban Council on a number of occasions.

THE FARM WOMEN, 1995. Wexford IFA supported the establishment of a Farm Family Group and the Farm Centre was packed by enthusiastic ladies from all parts of the county.

MINISTER FOR FOOD, 1995. Enniscorthy public representative John Browne became Minister for Food and one of his duties included climbing aboard a modern tractor. He was watched by David Butler (IFA Industry and Environment Chairman), Donal O'Leary, FBD, Cork, and the National President of IFA, Alan Gillis.

ROBERT CARLEY OWENS, c. 1941. He is shown in the uniform of the 12th Desmond Battalion of the Southern Command, in which he served during The Emergency in Cork, Limerick, Castleconnell and Templemore, before resigning his commission in 1944 with the rank of Battalion Adjutant. He succeeded his father, George Jackson Owens, as proprietor of Carley's Bridge Potteries, and developed the business over thirty-three years until his death in 1977 at the age of 62.